WOW
inventions
that changed the world

Philip Ardagh writes both fiction and non-fiction and is a familiar face at book festivals in England, Ireland, Scotland and Wales. His books have been translated into numerous languages, including Latin.

WOW inventions that changed the world

Philip Ardagh

Illustrated by Sally Kindberg

MACMILLAN CHILDREN'S BOOKS

First published 2000 by Macmillan Children's Books

This edition published 2006 by Macmillan Children's Books
a division of Macmillan Publishers Limited
20 New Wharf Road, London N1 9RR
Basingstoke and Oxford
Associated companies throughout the world
www.panmacmillan.com

ISBN 978-0-330-44454-5

3 5 7 9 8 6 4

A CIP catalogue record for this book is available from
the British Library.

Typeset by Nigel Hazle
Printed in China

For Frederick Ardagh,
the grandfather I never knew

CONTENTS

INVENTIONS!

Imagine a world where no one has discovered electricity . . . or a world where electricity has been discovered, but the inventors didn't know what to do with it! There would be no telephones, radios, televisions, computer games, internet . . . the list goes on and on. Think how different the whole history of the world would be without these, and other, great inventions. Without the invention of aeroplanes and, later, the jet engine, for example, a journey from Britain to Australia could take a very – and I mean *very* – long time. Now, nowhere in the world is more than 24 hours away in the fast planes. In this *WOW*, we take a look at some of the most fantastic inventions that changed the world, along with what led up to their invention and what came afterwards. As for what the future has in store, who knows? As these past inventions show, what seems impossible today could easily become a reality tomorrow. Just you wait and see or, better still, get inventing!

PHILIP ARDAGH

THE TELEPHONE

10 MARCH 1875, BOSTON, MASSACHUSETTS, USA

Scottish-born inventor Alexander Graham Bell is tired but excited. After years of work, he's ready to put his telephonic apparatus to the test. With his assistant, Thomas Watson, eagerly waiting by a second phone in the other room, Bell prepares himself for what he hopes will be a historic moment . . . but, then, disaster strikes. Acid from the battery powering his equipment spills on to his trousers and Bell leaps to his feet. 'Mr Watson! Come here! I want you!' he cries, unaware that he is speaking into the mouthpiece. He has just made the world's very first telephone call.

Alexander Graham Bell

Thomas Watson

A MARATHON RUN

How we can communicate with each other over distances further than a good yell can be heard is something that people have been puzzling over for a very long time indeed. One obvious solution was using runners. A runner could memorize an important message from one person and run off and repeat it to another. Once reading and writing were more widely developed, a runner could actually carry a written message. An ancient

3

Greek runner, sometimes referred to as Pheidippides, ran non-stop all the way from the Plain of Marathon to the city of Athens in 490 BC – over 37 km (23 miles) – with the message that the Athenians had defeated their Persian enemies in battle. He was so exhausted, he promptly dropped down dead, which was a shame. This exhausting run from Marathon is still remembered today, in marathon races (of nearly 42 km – over 26 miles).

DON'T SHOOT THE MESSENGER!

Other early runners, or messengers, often ended up dead for another reason: a tradition developed in some societies that deliverers of bad news should be killed. This was more than a teeny-weenie bit unfair – because they were just doing their jobs! – which is how we come to have the phrase 'Don't shoot the messenger'. (In other words, it's the *news* that's bad, not the poor person who brings it.)

A RIGHT ROYAL MALE

You can see how, over thousands of years, the system of messengers running here, there and everywhere with written messages developed into the postal service. In England, King Henry VIII (yes, he with the big belly and six wives) appointed a Master of the Post in 1516. These posts were 'staging posts', in other words they were places where a postmaster (usually an innkeeper) was responsible for passing a piece of mail on to the next post, and so on, down the line. And, in case you haven't guessed it, this is where we get the terms 'post office' and 'postage' from. (You can impress your friends by casually mentioning this in conversation.) Later, these staging posts became stop-off points for mail coaches, where the postman could rest or change his horses. Later still came postal workers with bicycles, vans, trains, ships and even aeroplanes.

GOT IT LICKED

The idea, in Britain, that a letter should cost the same to deliver wherever it was sent on the mainland came into being in 1840. Before that, the further a message went, the more you paid – which was bad luck if you lived in Cornwall and your granny lived somewhere in Scotland. At the same time, the world's first stick-on stamps were issued: the Penny Blacks. As their name suggests, they were black (with Queen Victoria's head on them in white) and cost an old penny each.

SMOKE AND FLAMES

But written messages delivered by others weren't the only way people could communicate without being face to face. Other obvious approaches included fires and smoke signals. A series of fires (called beacons) were lit around the coastline of England to warn of the coming of the Spanish Armada invasion force in 1588. When the ships were spotted and the alarm raised, a beacon was lit and, when the fire from that beacon was spotted by those at the next beacon, they lit theirs and so on. On the other hand, smoke signals – popularly used by some Native North Americans – could be used to send more complicated messages. Different puffs of smoke meant different things, so the receiver had to be able to 'read' them. Whereas a burning beacon signal meant just one pre-arranged thing – 'the enemy is coming!' – different smoke signals sent different messages.

FLAGGING IT UP

A popular system of ship-to-ship and ship-to-shore communications used to be flags. Traditionally, ships flew their country's flag so other ships would know whether they were friend or foe – and we all know what a skull-and-crossbones means – but other, smaller, shipboard flags were combined to make messages too. In battle, the flagship could hoist flags to send orders, which could be read through telescopes by those aboard other ships of the fleet. In one famous incident, at the battle of Copenhagen, Admiral Horatio Nelson was informed that the signal on the flagship was ordering withdrawal. Not wanting to quit fighting, he's said to have put his telescope up to his blind eye, and said, 'I really do not see the signal' – which was very naughty, but Nelson was a bit of an all-round hero and good guy, so history has decided that that's all right then! Flags are still used today, of course, but in friendlier 'battles', such as greeting the winner of a Grand Prix race with the chequered flag, or by linespeople at football and rugby matches, trying to catch the ref's eye.

IN A FLAP

Another, more complicated, system of signal-sending using flags, called semaphore, was developed. Here, whole messages could be spelled out letter by letter, with each letter formed by two flags being held out in particular positions. Short cuts were developed so, for example, a semaphore message from someone in big trouble and needing help could be shortened to SOS. The idea that it meant 'Save Our Souls' came later.

THE STARTING WIRE

All of the approaches mentioned so far were certainly impressive, but the real problem was the *time* it took to send a message over any great distance. All this was about to change with the invention of the telegraph – a way of sending coded electrical signals down a wire. (They weren't coded so that people couldn't understand them but

7

because it was assumed that a human voice couldn't be crammed down a telegraph wire, so the message had to be spelled out somehow.) A number of different people were working **independently** on the telegraph, with the first public telegraph lines being laid in England between Paddington and Slough in 1843 and in the USA between Washington DC and Baltimore, Maryland, in 1844. But it was the American inventor Samuel Morse, the 'father' of the telegraph, who turned it into such a brilliantly useful device.

ON THE DOT

It was Morse who invented Morse Code. (If his name had been Mr Cod it might have been called Cod Code.) In the same way that **software** is such an important part of computers, the way messages could be sent down the telegraph was what made the telegraph so successful. Instead of semaphore, Morse relied on electric dots and dashes to make up his alphabet. In Morse code, SOS started out

Morse Key for tapping out the messages

as three quick taps (or 'dots') for the 'S', followed by three slower 'dashes' for the 'O', followed by three quick 'dots' for the 'S' again. The dots and dashes were tapped out by the telegraph sender, sent electrically down the telegraph wire and picked up by the receiver in his headphones. (There were even competitions to see who could send and receive telegraphed Morse messages the quickest.) The world's first telegraphed Morse Code message was sent on

MORSE ALPHABET.

(INTERNATIONAL MORSE.)

Letters.

e	▪	f	▪▪■▪
t	■	l	▪■▪▪
i	▪▪	p	▪■■▪
a	▪■	j	▪■■■
n	■▪	b	■▪▪▪
m	■■	x	■▪▪■
s	▪▪▪	c	■▪■▪
u	▪▪■	y	■▪■■
r	▪■▪	z	■■▪▪
w	▪■■	q	■■▪■
d	■▪▪	ä	▪■▪■
k	■▪■	ö	■■■▪
g	■■▪	ü	▪▪■■
o	■■■	ch	■■■■
h	▪▪▪▪	é	▪▪■▪▪
v	▪▪▪■		

Numbers.

1	▪■■■■	6	■▪▪▪▪
2	▪▪■■■	7	■■▪▪▪
3	▪▪▪■■	8	■■■▪▪
4	▪▪▪▪■	9	■■■■▪
5	▪▪▪▪▪	0	■■■■■

Stops and Signs.

Period, or full-stop	▪▪▪▪▪▪	Hyphen	■▪▪▪▪■
Repeat, or interrogation	▪▪■■▪▪	Dash	■■■■■■
		Apostrophe	▪■■■■▪
		Parenthesis	■▪■■▪■

The Morse Code

9

24 May 1844 by Morse himself. It read: What hath God wrought! which was a bit serious, but this was a serious occasion. Just think about it. A message from Missouri to California that might take ten days to be delivered by the **Pony Express**, could now be delivered – zzzzzzzzip! – at the speed of light.

RING IN THE CHANGES

It was whilst experimenting with a telegraph machine that Alexander Graham Bell (1847–1922) developed the idea for a telephone – a machine that would convert speech into electrical energy, which could be sent great distances. A Scotsman, Bell moved to Canada and then the US in 1871. (He later became a US citizen.) In 1875, he founded a school in Boston, Massachusetts, for 'deaf-mutes' and was a speech teacher, fascinated by the human voice. (You can find out more about how a telephone actually works on page 14.) The phone wasn't his only invention either. He came up with the first electric hearing aid in 1846.

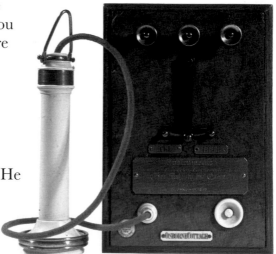

An early Bell telephone, 1877

MAKING A CASE

Amazingly, just a few hours after Bell had filed a **patent** for the telephone, another inventor by the name of Elisha Gray filed a claim that *he* had already invented a tele-

THE TELEPHONE.

An early ad for telephones

phone and that Bell shouldn't be given a patent. Various other inventors claimed to have invented the telephone before Bell too, but none of them could ever actually prove it in court! Poor old Bell had to defend his rights to the phone about 600 times before the Supreme Court of the United States finally officially pronounced, once and for all, that Bell did, indeed, invent it.

THE TELEPHONE REVOLUTION

It's not difficult to see how the telephone changed the world. Now, two people on opposite sides of the planet can talk to each other, without bleeps, dots, dashes, flashes or flags, and it's quick and easy. What could take months, can now take seconds. We can even 'fax' down phone lines, with a duplicate (or a **facsimile**) of an original document reproduced on a computer or fax machine anywhere in the world. Attach a modem to a modern computer and it converts the digital bits of a computer's output into an audio tone. Encoded as an electrical signal, this can then be decoded by a modem fitted to another computer at the receiving end. Hey presto! You've got email and everything the Internet has to offer (often wireless). As for mobile phones, over 800 million are now in use worldwide. We can use them just about any time, any place, anywhere. And they're not just for phone calls: you can email, surf the web, watch video, play games, listen to music, take pictures . . . The telephone has certainly earned its place in these pages.

RECORDED SOUND

DECEMBER 1877, MENLO PARK, NEW YORK, USA

Thomas Edison, already famous for many other inventions, sits himself down by a strange-looking contraption he has called the phonograph. Designed by him but built by his colleague John Kruesi, Edison is about to put the machine through another, early test. Placing his lips to the mouthpiece he recites the nursery rhyme 'Mary Had a Little Lamb'. Moments later, he plays the words back on the machine. He has managed to capture the human voice!

Thomas Edison

LOST AND GONE FOR EVER

Before writing, songs and stories were passed by word of mouth. You heard something. You tried to remember it. You repeated it and passed it on. Of course, you could never repeat it *exactly*. Then came writing. Now a song or a story could be written down. It could be read note for note and word for word. But, again, you could never repeat

someone else's version of a song or the way they spoke a story *exactly*. Once that moment of singing or speaking was gone, it was gone for ever. Even musical instruments are played differently by different musicians and no two performances by the same musician are ever identical.

THE MAGIC KEYBOARD

The Pianola, a special mechanical piano, was a brilliant invention of the 1890s because it actually played piano tunes *on a piano*. You could sit at home and listen to music coming out of your Pianola – with the keys moving before your eyes, as though being played by an invisible pianist! In fact, inside the Pianola, the keys were pressed down by air pressure from bellows. The airflow was controlled by perforations – small holes – in a large paper roll. As the roll moved, the air blew through the holes on to the right keys. Load the Pianola with a different paper roll, the air from the bellows would blow through different holes and different notes would play out a different tune. Magic!

GOOD VIBRATIONS

Sound is **vibration**. Speak into a telephone mouthpiece, to a friend, for example, and the **diaphragm** (a small, circular, very thin disc, pronounced 'dia-fram') vibrates, altering the magnetic field around a magnet, turning these vibrations into an electrical signal. This electrical signal passes down the phone wire, altering a magnetic field around a magnet in the receiver of your friend's phone, which in turn recreates the original vibrations in a diaphragm in their earpiece. And your friend hears your voice – all in a fraction of a second. Which is fiendishly clever and fiendishly simple, all at once!

EDISON ON THE CASE

Alexander Graham Bell had made the first phone call in 1875, but Thomas Edison (1847–1931) was working on an 'improved' version of the telephone in 1877. Watching a diaphragm vibrate, he wondered if it would be somehow possible to record those vibrations. He attached a **stylus** to the diaphragm so, when he spoke, the diaphragm would vibrate and make the stylus move up and down, creating tiny dents on a piece of paper. He tested this by saying the word 'Halloo!' Now he had the dents on the paper, he passed the paper back under the stylus, causing it to bob up and down and, in turn, make the diaphragm vibrate. In other words, he was trying to 'play' the sound he had recorded by simply reversing the process he'd used to record the dents on the paper. Although Edison was the first to admit that you needed 'strong imagination' to hear the original 'Halloo!', he could certainly hear something, and he knew that he was on to something *big*.

THE FIRST RECORDER

Rumours reached Edison that there were other inventors trying to come up with ways to record sound, so there was

15

no time to lose. When he designed the first phonograph, he decided that the stylus must make dents on a revolving cylinder covered in metal foil rather than paper. This should pick up the dents from the vibrations far more clearly. It worked! It worked! Soon, these metal foil cylinders were replaced by wax ones and phonographs sold the world over. (In Britain, they were called gramophones, and you still hear some older people talk about 'gramophone records' today.)

IT'S A RECORD!

The first machines to record and play flat discs, rather than cylinders, were invented in 1887 by Emile Berliner, who you'll find building a helicopter on page 77. (He was an engineer and inventor of many talents!) A needle attached to a diaphragm followed the tiny lumps and bumps in the grooves of the disc, or 'record', causing the diaphragm to vibrate down a metal tube, and the sound to come out – good and loud – from a horn-shaped loudspeaker. To make the needle follow the path of the groove, the record revolved on a wind-up turntable. Here was

A Berliner Gramophone, 1890

the first true record player, and it didn't even need electricity to make it work. By 1912, Edison himself had abandoned cylinders and switched to discs too.

DISCOGRAPHY

A Beatles LP recorded in vinyl, 1967

The first discs were called 78s. They had to go around 78rpm (**revolutions** per minute) for the sound to come out at the right speed, and were very brittle and heavy. They stayed in use right up until the 1950s, by which time long-playing records (or LPs) had become popular. LPs went round at a much slower 33.33rpm and were made of vinyl. They first appeared in about 1948. Later came 'singles' – small records, usually with a single track on each side, which revolved at 45rpm. By now, record players turned the turntables and amplified the sound electrically.

Gramophone and dog, c 1900

GETTING IT TAPED

The next big advance in sound recording to WOW everyone was the tape recorder. This records and plays back sound by recording electrical signals as magnetic

patterns on thin, magnetic oxide-coated plastic tape. When recording, a magnetic imprint is left on the tape as it passes a 'recording head'. When playing a tape, it passes a 'reproducing head' which turns this magnetic imprint into an electrical signal. The signal is then amplified and reproduced as sound. The great thing about tapes is that you can record over them again and again, something you can't do with records, and they don't break if you drop them! The first tape recorder was invented by a Danishman named Valdemar Poulsen in 1898. He called it a telegraphone.

SMALL IS BEAUTIFUL

For many years, tape recorders were big and bulky reel-to-reel machines, where tape unspooled from one reel on to another. Then, in the 1960s, came the far more convenient cassette recorder. The tapes for these machines came in a sealed

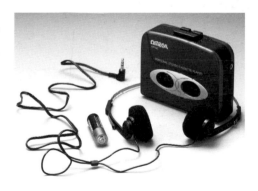

A personal stereo cassette player, c 1998

cassette with two tiny self-contained spools. In the late 1970s and early 1980s came personal stereos – tape players little bigger than the cassettes themselves.

19

A COMPACT SOLUTION

The 1980s also saw the Sony and Philips corporations develop the compact disc, introducing a whole new, mind-blowing level of sound quality. While record players use mechanics and tape recorders use magnetics, compact discs (often simply called CDs) use **optical** means to record and play. This breakthrough in technology has three big pluses: a whole lot of sound can be recorded on to one small disc, the sound quality is *fab* and the part which 'reads' the information from the disc doesn't actually touch it. Unlike a record worn down by a needle or a tape worn down by the 'heads', a CD is touched by light alone.

LASER TECHNOLOGY

Sound on a CD is recorded digitally. In other words, the audio signals are turned into a digital code made up of '0's and '1's. This digital code of the sounds then needs to be transferred to the disc. The disc has a light-sensitive base which is exposed to light from a laser that encodes the digital information – those '0's and '1's – on to the spinning disc. The disc is then dunked in a chemical that etches flat spots and pits (dents) into the areas exposed to the laser beam's digitally converted sound. Clever stuff, eh?

PLAYING A CD

Instead of a record needle, a CD player plays a compact disc using a laser scanner that reflects light off the top of it. If the light hits a flat spot, this represents a '0' in the digital code. If it hits a pit, this corresponds to a '1'. The CD player then simply converts these into electrical signals that can then be reproduced and amplified as music.

MP3 PLAYERS AND iPODS

Just a few years ago, iPods and MP3 players would have seemed like science-fiction fantasy: small portable music recorders and players that can store and play literally thousands of songs. And small really does mean small. Most are smaller than a pack of cards, some are slimmer than a CD case and others are even incorporated into mobile phones. Each player is made up of three basic components: the hard disc (storing the tracks as digital data), the circuit board (which translates the digital data into sound) and the battery (which powers it all). MP3s and iPods can be listened to through headphones when on the move, or through speakers when 'docked'. Music tracks can be downloaded off the Internet on to the machines. Now records of such downloads are incorporated into many 'Top 40' music charts along with (currently) more conventional CD sales. Things have come quite a long way since Edison recorded 'Mary had a little lamb' on to a revolving foil cylinder.

PHOTOGRAPHY

1839, LACOCK ABBEY, WILTSHIRE, ENGLAND

In his darkroom, Fox Talbot continues to make history. He may not be the first person to develop a photograph, but he's the first person to use this method – his method – and the results are remarkable. He smiles with real satisfaction as he watches the image appear before his eyes, like some ghostly apparition. One day, everyone will be able to take photographs, he muses . . . one day . . .

Fox Talbot (right) at the Reading Photographic Establishment, c 1848

AS IF BY MAGIC

A very early type of camera was the camera obscura, which was usually a building as well as a camera! A (bright) image of the view outside the building was projected on to a flat surface in the (dark) inside through a **convex** lens. The effect was amazing. Those inside the building, standing in the dark, could watch moving images of the world go by! Some artists drew around these projected images as the basis of their work so, even in an age before true photography, a camera helped them to make their finished paintings look so realistic. The word 'camera' actually comes from the Greek 'kamara',

A camera obscura, 1657

A 19th-century camera obscura advertisement

meaning vault – like the dark room, or vault, of the camera obscura.

HUMBLE BEGINNINGS

By the eighteenth century, it had been discovered that certain silver **compounds** were photosensitive – in other words, that, under certain conditions, they could create a photographic image. Using this information, the British scientists Sir Humphry Davy and Thomas Wedgwood began experiments with paper coated with silver chloride. They managed to produce basic images of silhouettes of leaves and people's profiles – faces sideways on – but these weren't proper, permanent photographs. When the paper was exposed to light, the whole print went black and the image was lost for ever.

AMAZING ADVANCES

The first true photographs weren't produced until the nineteenth century. They were taken and developed by the French physicist Joseph Nicéphore Niépce in 1822, again using silver chloride. In about 1829, he was partnered by the French painter Louis Daguerre. It was Daguerre who produced photographs on silver plates coated with a light-sensitive layer of silver iodide in 1839. After the plates had been exposed for a few minutes to the image he was photographing, he then used **mercury** vapours to develop a positive photographic image. At first, these too went black over time, until Daguerre 'fixed' the image by coating them with a solution of salt (which stopped the silver-iodide particles being sensitive to light). This 'fixing' method was originally invented by the British inventor William Henry Fox Talbot (1800–77), who was independently working on his own method of photography back in England. All early photographs were black and white, not colour, remember.

Joseph Nicéphore Niépce

An early 19th-century box-type camera obscura

A SENSATION!

Daguerre held an exhibition of his photographs, which he called daguerreotypes, in Paris in 1839. (No prizes for guessing where he got the idea for that mouthful of a name from.) Thousands flocked to see these magical images. The only problem was that they were one-off positive images on a silver plate. In other words, you couldn't take copies of the same picture. This didn't stop photographers setting up portrait studios everywhere, taking daguerreotypes of eager fee-paying members of the public.

A NEGATIVE IMPROVEMENT

Fox Talbot came up with his far more practical photographic approach, also in 1839. Because Daguerre's plates held positive images, everything that was dark in the photographed scene was dark on the plate (and everything light was light). The plate itself was the finished photo. With Fox Talbot's method, however, the plate held a negative image (where everything that was dark in the original photographed scene was now light, and everything light was dark). By shining light through this negative on to light-sensitive paper, where the light got through the light patches, it turned the paper dark, and where the light was blocked out by the dark patches, it left it light. This created a positive, life-like image. And, unlike Daguerre's single positive image plate, you could use one of Fox Talbot's negatives to make as many copies of the same photo as you wanted. And what did Fox Talbot call these types of photographs? Why, talbotypes, of course!

OTHER NAMES IN PHOTOGRAPHY

Other advances in photography came from people such as French physicist Claude Félix Abel Niépce de Saint-Victor. (You may need to pause for breath after reading such a long name.) In 1847, he came up with a way of making glass-plate negatives. These produced much cleaner, sharper images than Fox Talbot's grainy paper negatives. The trouble was, though, that the exposure – the length of time the camera shutter had to be open, exposing the image to the photographic plate – had to be much longer.

WET 'N' DRY

As time went on, various developments were made with both wet and dry photographic plates. The problem with wet plates was that they had to be both exposed and developed whilst they were still wet. This meant developing a photograph straight after it'd been taken. Because photographs have to be developed free from light, in darkrooms, this meant the darkroom needed to be nearby. *Very* nearby. So what happened if the photographer was miles from anywhere (on a battlefield in the American Civil War, for example)? The darkrooms came too, of course! Mobile horse-drawn darkrooms became all the rage. Fortunately, in 1878, the British photographer Charles Bennett invented a dry photographic plate – coated with a special emulsion of gelatine and silver bromide – which was very similar to the plates still used in photography today.

THE AMAZING MR MUYBRIDGE

One of the strangest people to be involved in early photography was Eadweard Muybridge. (He even changed the spelling of his name from Edward Muggeridge to the weird way you see here.) He became interested in photography when a horse breeder bet $25,000 that, when a horse was in full trot, all four of its hooves would leave the ground at the same time. (It was too fast to be sure with the naked eye.) Muybridge offered to take a series of photos to try to prove it for him. He lined one side of a racecourse with white paper (to create a clear background) and lined up a series of cameras along the other. Threads

Time-lapse photographs of a man riding a galloping horse

laid across the track were broken by the horse as it ran, releasing the cameras' shutters as it trotted through them. The result, in 1887, was a whole series of photos of the horse at different stages of its full trot. These included a picture that did, indeed, show the horse with all four hooves off the ground. You can find out more about Muybridge on page 36.

ROLL IN THE CHANGES

The really big advance, which suddenly made photography possible for the **masses**, was American George Eastman's invention of film-on-a-roll in 1884. This was a film made up of a long strip of paper coated with a sensitive emulsion. In 1889, he came up with the first transparent, flexible film – strips of cellulose nitrate – with the look and feel of modern film, and which easily loaded into a camera.

He *also* invented a small, easy-to-carry camera: the first Kodak box camera. In 1900, he started selling the even cheaper Kodak 'box' Brownie. Now everyone was taking pictures.

The Kodak Number 1 Brownie Camera in its box

HERE COMES COLOUR

Amazingly, the first colour photograph was produced as long ago as 1861, by the British physicist James Clerk Maxwell. The first colour glass plates went on the market in 1907. It wasn't until 1935 that Kodak produced its first colour film – positives that could be used to produce slides but not to make colour prints. Kodak colour negative film wasn't available until 1942 and wasn't widely used by amateur photographers in Britain until the mid-1960s. (Yes, when I was little, most people still took black-and-white photographs, and I'm not *that* old.) In 1947, Dr Edwin Land invented the Polaroid camera and instant photography was born.

Kodak counter display card for the Baby 'Brownie' Camera

LEAPS AND BOUNDS

One of the biggest changes in everyday photography, however, has been the arrival of the digital age. Not so long ago, most of us were all taking family snaps with cameras containing film, which we had to hand in, or send off, to be developed. Now, with far slimmer and less bulky digital cameras, we can store our pictures on computer, email them to friends or even print them out ourselves via a computer or straight to printer using a camera docking port or memory card. And we can edit the photos too, cropping, enhancing colour or even removing or adding objects and people. Digital cameras simply store the picture you've taken in a digital code of '0's and '1's, which are decoded as an image on your camera screen and, with the right software, your computer monitor.

3-D PICTURES

One of the most remarkable recent developments in photography, however, is the hologram. A hologram is a three-dimensional photograph, which means that the object in a hologram looks different when seen from different angles – front, left, right, above and below. A ghost in a hologram can appear to be leaping out of a wall right at you! (The word comes from the Greek 'holos', meaning 'whole' and 'gram', meaning 'message'.) The theory behind the technology to create such remarkable pictures was worked out by the British physicist Dennis Gabor as long ago as the Polaroid camera (1947), but wasn't developed until the 1960s, and wasn't wholly successful until the 1990s. Unlike an ordinary photo, holographic pictures are taken without using a lens. An object being 'photographed' for a hologram is illuminated by a laser beam of light, part of which is also reflected by a mirror or prism at a photographic plate. The shape of the object interferes with the light and it is the pattern of this interference that is recorded to create the 3-D holographic shape – and that's putting it simply! It's a complicated process with some remarkable results.

HERE, THERE, EVERYWHERE

Today, photographs are such a part of everyday life we hardly give them a second thought. There are photographs in newspapers and magazines, on advertising billboards, bus-shelter posters, in shop windows, and there are even glossy high-quality colour photos in family photo albums, or stored (without film) on our home computers. Fox Talbot wouldn't have believed his eyes . . .

CINEMA AND TELEVISION

26 JANUARY 1926, FRITH STREET, SOHO, LONDON, ENGLAND

Scotsman John Logie Baird nervously makes the final adjustments
to his prototype machine under the watchful eye of his invited
guests: members of the all-important scientific society, the Royal
Institution. They have come to Baird's home laboratory to see the
world's first demonstration of true television. Ready at last, the
expectant audience leans forward as one and . . . yes . . . there on
the screen is a moving, human face!

John Logie Baird in later life

THE FLICK OF A WRIST

Making pictures appear to move isn't the hardest thing in the world. If you hold this book by the spine in your left hand and flip the pages with your right, you'll see the picture of the aeroplane 'fly' across the bottom of the book. A similar principle was used to make moving-picture machines. When the viewer turned a handle, the machine flipped through a series of still photographs, giving the impression of movement. But these machines could only be watched by one viewer at a time. (These were often called 'What the Butler Saw' machines and showed naughty things a butler might have seen when peeping through a keyhole!)

Boys looking at mutascope machines on a pier, c 1930

A FLASH OF INSPIRATION

*Galloping horses on a
zoopraxiscope disc, 1893*

One of the earliest examples of a variation on this approach came from Eadweard Muybridge (who first showed up on page 28). He took a whole series of still photographs of horses trotting and galloping. He soon realized that if he was to flash one picture after another in quick succession, he could give the impression of the horse and rider moving before our very eyes. He manged this with an invention that he called the zoopraxiscope. A glass disc, showing pictures of the horse moving in sequence, was placed in front of a light projector and rotated between light flashes. The result was more of a horse 'running on the spot' than running off the screen, but it must have been most impressive. This was years before the invention of film projectors and certainly earns Muybridge a place in early cinema history.

THE WHYS AND WHEREFORES

The reason why these methods work is because of 'persistence of vision' – in other words, our eyes keep the visual image of the picture just gone (known as the 'positive after-image') while the next picture appears, so our brains are not aware of any gaps between the pictures. Up to a point, the more pictures (or 'frames') we see a second, the smoother and less flickering the images will seem. But our eyes need 0.2 seconds to receive an image and to transmit the information to our brains, so that we're aware of what we've seen.

EARLY DAYS

Before Muybridge's zoopraxiscope was the zoetrope, a more basic machine invented in the 1830s but working on the same principle. A series of still images were placed around the inside of an open-topped 'drum' with slits in its wall. When a person looked through the slits into the drum, and the drum was spun, the pictures whizzed past the viewer's eye quick enough to appear to be one continuous, moving image.

A zoetrope, c 1860

FIRST PROJECTIONS

By the 1870s, Frenchman Emile Reynaud had built a bigger, better zoetrope, with a reflector and a lens to enlarge the images. He even found a way of running a whole reel of images through the drum, rather than being limited to the number he could fix to the drum wall. This way, he could show hundreds of pictures – all drawings – running together to make one continuous moving 'picture show' lasting up to a quarter of an hour. He held screenings for the paying public at his Théatre Optique in Paris. In a sense, this was almost-but-not-quite the world's first cinema. He wasn't showing photographs.

MR EDISON JOINS THE FUN

In the late 1880s, Thomas Edison took the work of Muybridge, Eastman (see page 29) and others and gave one of his **employees** the job of coming up with a machine that would record moving pictures (by quickly taking one still picture after another) and another machine to show the results. That employee was the Englishman William Dickson and, by 1891, the result was a moving picture camera called a kinetograph and a viewing machine called a kinetoscope.

A man using an Edison kinetoscope, c 1894

FRAME BY FRAME

The camera – the kinetograph – had a motor that moved the roll of celluloid film past the lens where it was exposed to light and each single picture was taken. If the developed film was then shown on the kinetoscope projector at the same speed, the image would appear to move naturally. It was soon decided that motors made cameras heavy and difficult to lug about. These were soon replaced with much lighter and more mobile hand-cranked cameras. The most ingenious part of Dickson's invention was its **sprocket** mechanism. It was this that stopped the film in the right place for each exposure, or frame, to be taken. In these early days, different cameras used different speeds, so films had to be played back at different speeds too. And there was no sound to go with the pictures back then.

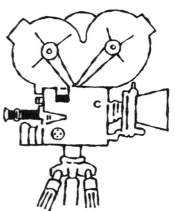

ALMOST THERE

Early moving films were often referred to as 'motion pictures' and people (particularly Americans) still speak of the 'motion-picture industry' today. The word 'movies' – as in pictures-which-move – is still used to mean films. Edison built his own motion-picture studio in the grounds of his Menlo Park laboratory in 1893. Later that year, he

gave a public showing of the films that he'd shot but – unlike Emile Reynaud's Paris screenings, where the Frenchman projected his moving drawings on to screens at his Théatre Optique – only *one* member of the public at a time could view the moving photographs!

Lumière brothers projector from 1896

The viewer had to watch it through a tiny window on the front of the kinetoscope. But, crazy though this might seem today, this didn't stop kinetoscope 'viewing parlours' from cropping up in US cities in 1894.

THE BIRTH OF MODERN CINEMA

Although Edison may not have been too pleased about it, the French brothers Auguste and Louis Lumière are credited by most people as the founders of true cinema in 1895 – so much so that, in 1995, many people celebrated 100 years of cinema. (It was the Lumières who came up with the term 'cinématographe' from which we get 'cinema'.) The Lumières ran a photographic equipment

Louis Lumière in later life

40

factory in Lyons and, by 1895, had not only developed a better, lighter, hand-held movie camera based on the idea of Edison's kinetograph, but had also invented a way of projecting the image on to a screen. After a number of test screenings for small, invited audiences, the first public screening took place in Paris in December 1895.

ACROSS THE GLOBE

Since Edison's invention, things were moving quickly the world over. In Germany, brothers Emil and Max Skladanowsky had invented their own projector and had screened films in Berlin as early as November 1895. In

Filming the 1895 Derby for screening

Britain, Birt Acres and Robert Paul were projecting films by January 1896. Back in America, a projector called the Vitascope was developed and its inventors teamed up with Edison to go into production. What makes the Lumière brothers so special, though, is that they not only developed the camera and the projector but also made very memorable short films to show off their inventions – everything from comedies to documentaries.

BIGGER! NOISIER! IN COLOUR!

Early films had to fit on one reel and lasted about 10 to 12 minutes. Improved technology meant that films could get longer. 'Talkies' (films with soundtracks, where you could actually hear people speak) arrived in the 1920s. To begin with, there were two systems. One was where the sound was recorded on to disc, and this record was played as the film was screened. The second was to record the soundtrack directly on to the celluloid film strip (which is how they are recorded today). The earliest colour films relied on special filters being placed over the projection lens. The first full-length colour film that didn't rely on this approach, but used a system called two-colour Technicolor, was made in 1922. The first film to use the improved three-colour Technicolor was a short Walt Disney cartoon called *The Trees and the Flowers*. The first feature-length cartoon was also by Walt Disney: *Snow White and the Seven Dwarfs*. Colour didn't become standard until the 1950s, when cinema had a new rival: television.

THE SPINNING DISC

Different countries have different ideas as to who it was who invented television, but the world's first commercially transmitted TV pictures were transmitted by Scottish-born John Logie Baird (1888–1946). At the heart of his invention was a mechanical device called 'Nipkow's Disc' and the (then) latest in electronics. The disc, named after German engineer Paul Nipkow, who invented it in 1884, was an upright disc – up on end, not flat like a CD – punched with a carefully ordered spiral pattern of holes. Placed in front of an object, the disc was spun. As it spun, the first hole passed across the top of the object, the second passed across the object a fraction lower down, and so on. In one complete revolution, the disc's holes had 'scanned' the entire object. If a camera filmed these scanned images through the disc and electronically transmitted them to a receiver that shone light through a similar disc, Baird reasoned, then surely a picture of the object could somehow be recreated on an electronic screen at the other end? Though trained as an engineer, poor health meant that Baird had to earn his money doing odd jobs whilst experimenting and inventing in his spare time. Apart from a few lenses and the motor, his prototype was made from household objects, including an old tea chest, with Nipkow Discs cut from an old hat box, a biscuit tin and a darning needle. Most of it was held together with sealing wax and string!

TV'S BASIC BEGINNINGS

In 1925, Baird was ready to put his contraption to the test. He sat a ventriloquist's dummy at one end of his London attic and prepared – fingers crossed – to transmit black-and-white pictures of it on to his television at the other. The image was scanned using a spinning Nipkow Disc, with a light-sensitive tube electronically recording the amount of brightness or darkness coming through each one of the particular thirty holes as it spun. This information was then turned into elec-trical signals that were transmitted to the receiver

'Stookie Bill', Logie Baird's television dummy, c 1923

– the television set – which contained another Nipkow Disc, this time with a lamp behind it. The signals from the light-sensitive tube in the transmitter controlled how light or dark a lamp should be, shining light through the holes of the disc. This way, it recre-ated how light or dark the original image of the dummy had been when scanned through the different holes – and built up the result on a screen of thirty electronic lines, one for each hole in the disc. The result? Hey presto: flickery, black-and-white tele-vision pictures of the dummy. Crude, but television pictures nonetheless.

SOME TV FIRSTS

Now he needed a live, moving subject! Baird was so excited, he rushed out and found a boy called William Taynton to take the dummy's place. That afternoon, Baird repeated the experiment. The result was the world's first moving television pictures! In January 1926, Baird showed his 'television' to the public. In 1927, he sent a television picture – the signals from the light-sensitive tube to control the brightness of the lamp shining through the Nipkow Disc – down the phone line between London and Glasgow, so building up a picture of shades of grey on a TV screen at the other end. A year

A Baird television receiver from 1936

later, he sent a picture across the Atlantic. By 1929, the BBC – the British Broadcasting *Company*, back then, not Corporation – started to transmit the world's first commercial television programmes using Baird's invention, but only occasionally! (Their main interest was radio.) By 1932, regular broadcasts were scheduled.

THE FALL AFTER THE RISE

But, however great his original achievements, John Logie Baird's success was short-lived. By 1936, his mechanical approach was outdated and replaced by less cumbersome all-electrical methods of transmitting and receiving images. (Out went the discs, in came a method of directly scanning and transmitting the electrical pattern of an image.) This was based on the Russian-born American Vladimir Zworykin's work in the USA, on both TV cameras and picture tubes. Having been the birth of television, Baird's work had already become **obsolete**.

STILL A BRILLIANT MIND

Baird may have been downhearted, but he never gave up. His contribution to TV didn't end there. In 1938, he

John Logie Baird and his TV apparatus, Science Museum, 1926

arranged the world's first public showing of colour television in front of an audience of 3,000 at the Dominion Theatre, London. The screen was 12 feet by 9 feet! He also invented a system of 3-D TV, and even a method of recording TV programmes many, many, many years before the arrival of the video!

'INFINITY AND BEYOND!'

Today, we live in a world of hundreds of television channels, transmitted by a whole variety of means: beamed across the world by **satellites** orbiting the Earth, from cables underground or by analogue and digital transmissions, received by dish or aerial. We can record and watch films and television programmes with DVD recorders (replacing the old video recorders), and digital technology means even clearer pictures and sound quality, further enhanced by a new breed of High Definition televisions. In 1995, *Toy Story* created a stir as the first full-length feature film to be made without cameras. It was entirely animated on computer using CGI (Computer Generated Imagery). In such a short space of time since then, such techniques have become commonplace. We even take for granted the fact that events can be beamed from around the globe, live into our living room. Film and television have completely changed our world!

RAILWAYS

OCTOBER 1829, RAINHILL, ENGLAND

The Rainhill Trials are at an end. The competition to see who wins the £500 prize and whose steam locomotive will be built in factories to pull the trains on the new Liverpool to Manchester line are over. Five locomotives entered, only three worked well enough to stay in the running — and there will be only one winner. Robert Stephenson turns to his father George, on the footplate of the *Rocket*. He smiles nervously. Surely, they must have won. Surely?

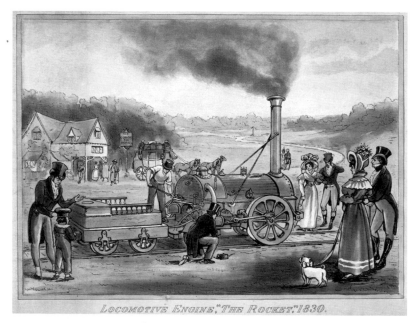

Stephenson's Rocket, *1830*

LEGGING IT

Before the invention of the steam locomotive, the quickest way to get around on land was by horse. Trains were invented before cars and planes so, before trains, what we think of as a quick trip today could have taken days! By far the most common transport in Europe was walking-on-your-own-two-feet. Some people owned their own horses, others travelled in stage coaches. A coach journey across Britain could be a very bumpy, cold and uncomfortable ride, taking days, with overnight stops at coaching inns.

ON THE RAILS

The first wagons to be pulled along rails were pulled by horses, not locomotives. About 250 years ago, some miners discovered it was much easier to get their (very heavy) wagons of iron and coal from their mine and down to the port on rails. For the downward trip, a man rode on the back of the full wagon, controlling the speed with a brake. The horse would then pull the empty wagon, still guided by the rails, back up the hill to the mine.

GOING NOWHERE

Steam engines were also first designed for mines, but not *moving* steam engines (in other words, not locomotives). One of the earliest uses for steam was to power the pumps that took the water out of the mines, deep below the ground. (The first of these engines was built by Englishman Thomas Newcomen in 1712.) So some mines had rails, and some had static steam engines, but no one had yet thought of putting the two together and coming up with steam engines pulling wagons on rails.

A Newcomen Engine from 1752

FROM DANGEROUS BEGINNINGS . . .

By the end of the eighteenth century, Scotsman James Watt had improved these earlier versions of static steam engines, but thought that a steam locomotive would be far too dangerous. In 1769, a Frenchman called Captain Nicholas Cugnot had WOWed a crowd of onlookers with a steam carriage that reached an amazing two to three miles an hour, before crashing and blowing up! The French authorities dragged away both him and what was left of his machine. Cugnot was jailed!

speed limit 2mph

WHAT, NOT WATT?

Two common **misconceptions** are that James Watt was the first to see the great possibilities in the power of steam and that George Stephenson built the first steam locomotive. Well, we've already seen that Thomas Newcomen beat Watt to it – and, in fact, a Greek inventor called Hero beat them *both* to it in Egypt over 2,000 years ago, with a steam-powered spinning ball – and we're about to see Stephenson beaten by one Richard Trevithick.

GETTING BETTER ALL THE TIME

Richard Trevithick, the son of a manager of a Cornish tin mine, built his first full-sized steam locomotive in 1801, though he had tried a few smaller models with some success before then. Instead of running on rails it ran on the road or, more to the point, it very quickly ran *off* the road – straight into some poor, unsuspecting person's house! In 1804, Trevithick was at it again. To win a bet with the owner of an iron works, he built a second locomotive – one that pulled a 10-tonne load down a 16 km (10-mile) track.

CATCH ME WHO CAN

Trevithick's greatest triumph was his locomotive the *Catch Me Who Can*. In 1808, he built a circular track in London and the locomotive steamed around and around it all day. The clever part was that the track was surrounded by a high wooden fence. This meant that the public could hear

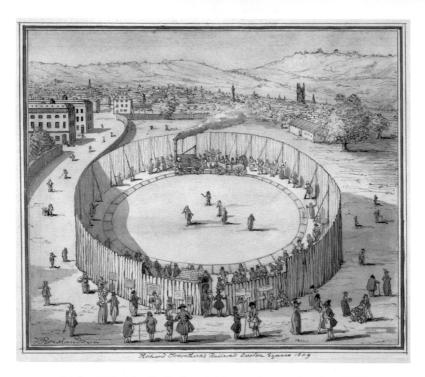

Richard Trevithick's Railroad, Euston Square, London, 1809

the noise and see the smoke from the locomotive's funnel, but the only way they could get to see it was to pay a one-shilling entrance fee – and pay it plenty of people did, even though a shilling was a lot of money in those days.

LET DOWN

What eventually caused the *Catch Me Who Can* track to close down was the same thing that stopped steam trains becoming a way of getting around in the early 1800s. The tracks weren't strong enough for the train. They kept on breaking. Wood was too weak for constant use, and the iron of the late eighteenth and early nineteenth centuries was too brittle: it snapped too easily. It was only when cast iron – an iron so strong that it had to be moulded into shapes when a molten liquid – came along that steam railways became a reality.

THE STEPHENSONS

Robert Stephenson   *George Stephenson*

Though not the first names in steam locomotive history, the Stephensons – George and son Robert – are two of the most famous. George Stephenson got a job in a **colliery** and one of the most important things in a colliery was moving all that coal. Like many colliery owners, George's boss, Nicholas Wood, thought that steam trains would be an excellent way of transporting such heavy loads, and George Stephenson's job was to build them. In 1825, the world's first public railway opened in England, between Stockton and Darlington. Although most of the carriages were pulled along the track by horses, sometimes a

The opening of the Stockton & Darlington Railway, 1825

locomotive called the *Locomotion* was used. Built by George Stephenson, it could pull wagons jam-packed with hundreds of excited people (many just along for the ride), along with tonnes of cargo – all at an impressive speed of five miles an hour.

STEPHENSON'S ROCKET

Then, in 1829, came the Rainhill Trials. Of the four locomotives that started the competition, the *Perseverance* didn't **persevere**, because it didn't have enough power, the *Sans Pareil* (French for 'Without Equal') used up huge amounts of fuel and broke down after its eighth run, and

Remains of the Stephenson's 'Rocket', 1829

the *Novelty* – a popular choice with the crowds – kept on grinding to a halt. Which left Stephenson's *Rocket*. It steamed along the test track at an average speed of 23 km (14 miles) an hour and was a huge success. On 15 September 1830, the Liverpool and Manchester line opened, with Stephenson's trains. Unfortunately, the local MP, William Huskisson, stepped on to the track and was hit by the *Rocket*! He was the first person to be killed on a public railway!

PROBLEMS AND IMPROVEMENTS

Soon after this, improvements to steam trains and tracks came thick and fast, and the famous engineer Isambard Kingdom Brunel built his Great Western Railway. It wasn't until 1892, though, that a standard gauge (width of track) was agreed so that all trains could run on all tracks! Before that, George Stephenson's gauge was 1,435 mm (4 feet 3½ inches) wide, whilst Brunel's gauge was 2,133 mm (7 feet) wide. The one Stephenson used became standard. Some people, meanwhile, hated everything about the railways, which were noisy, smelly, dirty, cut through people's land and put many stage-coach companies out of business – so it's hardly surprising really.

OPENING UP AMERICA

On the plus side, the steam railway opened up continents. In the past, people had set up home along rivers and roads. Now, in countries such as the USA, people were setting up along 'railroad tracks', with telegraph lines set up alongside them. With more and more people from Europe settling in the USA, more and more people moved out west and the railways soon followed, spreading out in a network across much of this vast country. On 10 May 1869, the USA was linked from the west coast to the east when the Central Pacific and Union Pacific lines joined at a place named Promontory Point. There were big celebrations! Two of the biggest problems on early American railroads, though, were attacks from thieves (many of whom specialized in robbing trains) and from Native North Americans who didn't like the trains passing through their ever-shrinking lands.

NEW SOURCES OF POWER

Apart from the noise and the soot from the belching smoke, steam trains used up *huge* amounts of coal to heat the fire to create the steam to power the engines, so engineers and inventors looked for new ways of powering locomotives. Dr Rudolf Diesel invented what became known as the diesel engine in 1892, powered by diesel (a kind of petrol), and the discovery and harnessing of electricity made this an obvious source of power too. By the 1930s, more and more diesel and electric locomotives were being made. By the 1950s, steam-powered trains were coming to an end in Europe.

FASTER AND CLEANER

In countries with little coal, such as Switzerland, electric locomotives made a huge difference. The 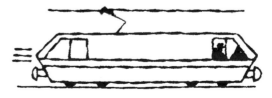 power usually comes from overhead cables but can also come from a third electrified rail. In Britain, most mainline trains are pulled by diesel-electric locomotives. The engine itself is diesel but it powers an electric generator that, in turn, powers electric motors that turn the wheels.

UNDERGROUND, OVERGROUND

The world's first underground railway opened in London in 1863 (but took a long, long time to grow to be anywhere near the size it is today). In 1900, this was followed by the Paris metro in France and the New York subway in the USA. Today, we even have a train tunnel under the English Channel, joining Britain to the Continent. Meanwhile, above the streets are electric monorail trains – running on a single, central rail – and, in England in 1984, they even began running trains that float above their tracks using electromagnets. To the Stephensons, it would have seemed like magic.

CARS! CARS! CARS!

MAY 1902, BEXHILL-ON-SEA, EAST SUSSEX, ENGLAND

The 8th Earl De La Warr, in conjunction with the Automobile
Club of Great Britain and Ireland, has arranged the first
motor racing on British soil, with cars speeding, rattling and
belching to and from Galley Hill, along the seafront. And the
winner? Beating a huge number of entrants, including Lord
Northcliffe – the founder of the *Daily Mail* newspaper – in
his Mercedes, is Monsieur Leon Serpollet of France, reaching
the staggering speed of 54 miles per hour in his steam-
powered car, the *Easter Egg*!

A WHEEL, FOR STARTERS

We don't know who invented the wheel but we do know
that not all societies used it to get around. The Aztecs –
famous for their pyramid temples, blood sacrifices and
being wiped out by their Spanish conquerors
– had no carts or trucks. They had no
beasts of burden, either, come to that.
They walked or ran everywhere. In other
cultures, however, people went from
walking to riding to pulling carts to sitting in
carts and coaches, and many went on to
steam trains and, eventually, motor cars.

59

DOOMED TO FAIL

The earliest experiments with 'horseless carriages' relied on the power of the wind. A 'sailing wagon' built in the Netherlands in 1599 looked like a small sailing ship on wheels! Sailing ships had long been the fastest, biggest and most effective form of transport for thousands of years – but sails weren't so useful on land. For a start, the wind had to be blowing in the direction you wanted to drive, and the roads would have to be very smooth indeed. Like the 'windmill' and kite-powered cars, which were also suggested, the sailing wagon was of no use whatsoever!

BUILDING UP STEAM

In 1769 came Cugnot's explosive steam carriage (which you can read about on page 50) but, again, it had its serious faults. Some of the most successful early cars were made by Richard Trevithick of steam-train fame so, not surprisingly, his cars were powered by steam. The first, built in 1801, got the nickname 'Captain Dick's Puffer'. The second, bigger version of 1803 raised more than a few eyebrows as it steamed through the streets of London. Soon, passenger-carrying steam coaches were driving around the roads, but they never

Richard Trevithick's London Road Carriage

A Stanley Steamer, 1899

really caught on in Europe. In the USA, it was a different matter. Steam coaches – and later steam cars – caught on in a big way. The *Stanley Steamer*, built in the USA by twins Freelan and Francis Stanley, set a world land speed record of a staggering 195.64 km (121.57 miles per hour) in 1906!

INTERNAL COMBUSTION ENGINE

There were many reasons for not liking steam cars, not least because you needed a furnace and boiler on board, which was a bit like driving around with a bomb! All this changed with the invention of the internal combustion engine, a remarkable invention that was to introduce motoring to the masses. Instead of steam from heated water pushing a piston down a cylinder to turn the wheels, inside an internal combustion engine, a spark ignites gas (or, later, petrol **vapour**) to do the same. (That's what spark plugs are for; so now you know, if you didn't already, that is.) This made engines much smaller and more effective – no need for those big boilers of piping hot water or for furnaces! Few experts can agree on who actually invented the internal combustion engine, but the first person to use one in a car was J. J. Lenior, a Belgian in Paris. His gas-powered car took two hours to travel 9.7 km (6 miles) – an average of 4.9 km an hour. In 1875, the Austrian Siegfried Marcus built a petrol-powered car. Surprisingly, neither Lenior nor Marcus tried to improve on their ideas. Perhaps they thought they'd made their car as good as cars could get to be. If so, they were sadly mistaken, as Mr Gottlieb Daimler and Mr Karl Benz were about to prove.

EARLY CARS

Karl Benz built the first really successful, widely purchased car in 1885. It had a lightweight frame, with two big bicycle-type wheels at the back and one at the front. He called it the Motorwagen. Unlike Benz's car, Daimler's first vehicle, built a year later, was really a carriage designed to be attached to a horse, but converted to a car, with an engine added! Ten years later, many cars still looked like carriages. The 1896 Peugeot had a cosy passenger compartment, but the driver had to sit *outside*, just as he would on a horse-drawn coach! Cars were soon all the rage and, in 1898, the Benz Viktoria was put through its paces at the London Motor Show, driving up ramps and down steps to prove just how nifty it could be!

A Benz 1.5 hp motor car, 1888

A RUBBERY IDEA

The success of the car owes a great deal to the rubber pneumatic – air-filled – tyre. Pneumatic tyres absorb a lot of the lumps and bumps of the road, so we're not shaken around in our cars. The American inventor Charles Goodyear discovered a process called vulcanization in 1839. This made rubber less sticky, much tougher and more elastic. In 1845, Scotsman Robert Thomson patented a basic pneumatic tyre. It was in 1888, though, that another Scotsman, John Boyd Dunlop, invented the rubber pneumatic tyre similar to those used today. (Legend has it, he was experimenting with water-filled tyres, when his neighbour suggested he try air!)

ELEGANCE AND LUXURY

Gottlieb Daimler not only made Daimler cars but was soon building Mercedes with an engineer called Maybach. Right up until 1906, Mercedes were thought to be the very best cars, but then along came Mr Charles S. Rolls and Mr Henry Royce. Aristocratic car fanatic Rolls is supposed to have said to Royce, 'You make the cars, I'll sell them, and we'll call it the Rolls-Royce.' The engine of a Rolls-Royce was so quiet that it was said to purr, and so well-built that it needed very little attention. (In 1926, Daimler and Benz's companies joined together to produce Mercedes-Benz cars.)

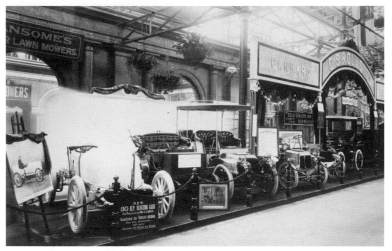

Charles S. Rolls & Co.'s stand at Britain's first motor show,
Crystal Palace, 1903

'SO LONG AS IT'S BLACK'

Another famous phrase in the history of the car is
American car-maker Henry Ford's line: 'You can have it
any colour you want so long as it's black.' He was referring
to his 1908 car, the Model T Ford, and the reason why each
and every Model T had to be black was because it was the
first car in the world to be mass-produced. Ford may not
have invented the motor car, but he invented the assembly
line. Each worker spent every day performing the same
task on a car, in the same place on the assembly line, before
it went down to the line to the next person, and so on, right
down the line until the car was fully assembled, sprayed
black and ready to drive out of the factory. The Model T
Fords, nicknamed 'Tin Lizzies', were cheap, reliable and
an *enormous* success. In 1922, the Ford Motor Company
became the first car manufacturer to make over a million

cars in one year, and by 1927 it had sold over 15 million Model Ts.

A Model T Ford motor car, 1916

FAMILY FAVOURITES

Today, cars are accepted as an everyday part of most people's lives, but some cars stick out from all the rest. Two of the best-loved cars, with the most loyal following, are the Volkswagen Beetle and the Mini. The Volkswagen, meaning 'People's car', was first produced in Germany in 1938. This was when the Nazi dictator Adolf Hitler was in power, and he loved these cars. He even laid the foundation stone of the original Volkswagen factory! Despite its early connection with Hitler, when production of the original Beetle finally stopped in 1978, over 19.75 million had been made, which was certainly a world record. The Mini, another small car as the name suggests, was British and first rolled off the production line in 1959.

FLOPS?

Not all advances or makes of car have been rip-roaring successes. In 1958, the Ford Edsel was launched, with a pair of huge grilles on the front. What the designers had thought looked exciting and modern, the car-buying public thought looked ugly. Most Edsels stayed in the showrooms. When the company stopped producing Edsels just a year later, they'd lost $250 million! Another disaster, smaller in every way, was British inventor Sir Clive Sinclair's tiny electric car, the C5. He argued that it was economical, environmentally friendly and nippy in traffic. Many people seemed to think it was just plain silly! In fact, the first electric car was invented by a Belgian in 1899 and electric cars were a common sight in the US, right up until 1930. Because they do, indeed, cause less pollution, there's renewed interest in electric vehicles – but probably not ones quite so small and close to the ground as the C5.

SAFETY

Today, safety is all-important in car design – mainly safety for those people *inside* the car. Seat belts hold the driver and passenger in place and some vehicles even have built-in child seats. Airbags automatically inflate if a car stops suddenly or hits an object. Cars are given side-impact bars to protect occupants from side-on collisions. But now there is mounting pressure for cars to be designed to minimize harm to **pedestrians** in an accident. There are also suggestions that all cars' speeds be controlled by satellite, preventing people from breaking the speed limit. Some specially adapted cars are designed to slow down if they are too close to the car in front, or even not to start if the driver has been drinking alcohol!

FREEDOM?

How have cars changed the world? Immeasurably. Places that were inaccessible even to the railway can be reached by car. Without having to rely on public transport and timetables, people can now go where they want, when they want and, often, considerably faster than they could on foot or horseback . . . except, of course, in traffic jams. In some cities, during rush hour, the average speed of a car is slower than the average speed of a horse taking the same route a hundred years ago! Horse riders weren't stuck behind a long line of other horses, waiting at the traffic lights! Add to that the pollution, noise and road deaths, and one's reminded that – as with most inventions that have had such an impact on our world – there are disadvantages as well as advantages to living in the motor age.

AEROPLANES

17 DECEMBER 1903, KITTY HAWK, NORTH CAROLINA, USA

Wilbur and Orville Wright, c 1910

The two brothers have taken it in turns. Yesterday, the toss of a coin decided that Wilbur would be the first to pilot their new, improved *Flyer* but his take-off had been too steep and the plane had crashed. Today, it is Orville's turn and he's flying! He's FLYING! After covering 37 metres (121ft) he's now coming in to land. He's about to successfully complete the world's first aeroplane flight!

UPS AND DOWNS

Ever since the first humans watched birds soaring through the skies, people have wanted to fly. The ancient Greek myth of Icarus tells of how he flew too close to the sun with his wings made of wax and bird feathers and how, when the wax melted in the heat, he plummeted into the sea. (His dad, Daedelus, was far more sensible and flew to safety – but this was all just make-believe, anyway.) When an English monk called Eilmer covered his arms and legs with bird feathers and jumped from the tower at Wiltshire Abbey in the eleventh century, he didn't fly *or* die. But he did manage to break both legs.

AS HIGH AS A KITE

There are reports that, in fifth-century China, people tried strapping themselves to giant kites, with ropes firmly tethering them to the ground. This wasn't so much a way of getting about but of getting a good view, and there's nothing said about what happened if the wind suddenly dropped – *splat* probably.

AN IMPORTANT CONCLUSION

In the thirteenth century, *another* English monk (a chap called Roger Bacon, this time) conducted a series of studies that led him to believe that air could support a heavier-than-air craft in the same manner that water supports boats. How right he was.

HEAD IN THE CLOUDS

Then, in the early sixteenth century, along came Leonardo da Vinci, painter, architect, sculptor, musician, engineer, scientist, *inventor* and all-round, grade-one genius. He was fascinated with the idea of human flight and, amongst other things, came up with the idea for three different types of heavier-than-air aircraft. These were the ornithopter (a machine with mechanical wings that were supposed to flap

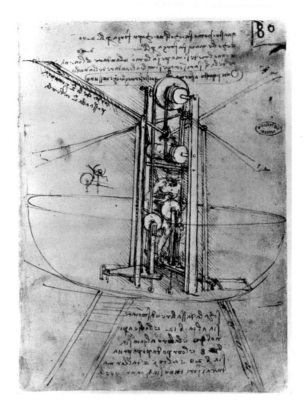

*Leonardo da Vinci's late 15th-century
design for a flying machine*

like a bird's), a helicopter – yes, I did say helicopter – and a glider (with fixed wings that would enable the pilot to coast on the air).

BACK TO THE DRAWING BOARD

These were only ever drawings on paper and, had he built them as he'd designed them, they'd never have flown, but helicopters and gliders were certainly the right idea, anyway. And, oh yes, he did invent the **propeller** *and* came up with the idea for the **parachute**. The first practical parachute, however, wasn't invented until the 1780s.

JUMP!

A Frenchman by the name of Jean Pierre Blanchard dropped a dog wearing a parachute from a great height in 1785. (I don't know what name the dog went by, as it went by.) It wasn't until eight years later – in 1793 – that Blanchard himself gave it a go and claimed to be the first person to have made a successful parachute jump. Note the word 'successful', allowing for all those people who might possibly have taken the plunge, but whom – aaaaaaaaah! – didn't live to tell the tale.

MORE THAN JUST HOT AIR

The reason why Blanchard was able to drop the dog from a great height was because he was an aeronaut: he flew in hot air balloons. The principle was simple: hot air rises, so fill a balloon 'envelope' with hot air and the balloon will rise. Attach a basket (called a gondola) to the balloon, with you inside it, and *you* will rise too. These lighter-than-air balloons were the first truly successful means of people taking to the skies. The first successfully flown balloon was built by two French brothers, Joseph and Etienne Montgolfier, and was flown across Paris in 1783 by François Pilâtre de Rozier (a scientist) and the Marquis d'Arlandes. They carried a sponge and bucket on board, just in case the craft caught fire. Suddenly, ballooning was all the rage.

SHIPS OF THE SKIES

The next step from balloons filled with hot air (which had to be continually heated from a burner positioned at an opening at the bottom of the envelope) was to airships with envelopes filled with sealed-in lighter-than-air gases. The first airship flight was piloted by Frenchman Henry Giffard in 1852, but the golden age of airships didn't begin until 1900. Amazing aircraft though they were, their frames

The Giffard Airship, 1852

73

were fragile (because they had to be so light) and could be easily damaged in storms, and the hydrogen gas inside them could be very dangerous, as in *boom*! Airships went out of fashion in 1937 after the giant Zeppelin airship, the *Hindenberg*, crashed in a mass of flames – a horrific accident that was caught on **newsreel**.

GLIDING BY

Leonardo da Vinci may have come up with the idea for a glider, but the first real glider was piloted by . . . er . . . by a ten-year-old boy in 1849. The glider was built by Englishman Sir George Cayley when he was seventy-six, using the hull of an old boat for the glider's body. It was towed into the air on the end of a rope, like a giant kite. Cayley inspired the German engineer Otto Lilienthal, who became the glider expert of his day. Tragically, Lilienthal died in 1896 after breaking his back in a test flight – but not before he, in turn, had inspired two American brothers who owned a number of bicycle shops: Orville and Wilbur Wright.

ON THE WRIGHT TRACK

The famous 'Wright brothers', Wilbur (1867–1948) and Orville (1871–1912) did, in fact, have two brothers and a sister, but they're the two Wright brothers who are famous because they're the ones who changed the world. They were friends of fellow American Octave Chanute who built and flew many gliders – but they were interested in *powered* flight: flight where it was the aircraft that moved itself forward, rather than simply being carried by the air. To do this, they would need an aircraft of the right shape and weight, an engine turning a propeller to give the plane **lift** to take it off the ground and thrust to make it go forwards. They started off with gliders, though, building and test-flying them at the windswept sand dunes of Kitty Hawk, a fishing village in North Carolina.

REAL PLANES AT LAST

Orville and Wilbur finally decided that a powered plane couldn't simply be a glider with an engine on it. They eventually came up with the *Flyer*, with longer, narrower wings and movable tail fins, like the rudder of a ship. Next,

The Wright Brothers' first attempt at powered flight, 14 December 1903

they tested different shapes and sizes of home-made propeller, which would 'suck in' the air, pulling it (and the *Flyer*) forward and giving it lift, if everything went to plan. But was it ready to fly?

MAKING A SPLASH

On 8 December 1903, Professor Samuel Langley, head of the famous Smithsonian Institution in America, launched his own aircraft, *Great Aerodrome*, for the second time. Fired from a catapult on top of a specially converted houseboat on the Potomac River, it fell straight into the water . . . just as it had the first time. Failure though it was, the Wright brothers knew that the race was now on to be the first to fly. And, on 17 December 1903, they were. The *Flyer* worked – their whole design of wing shape, hull and propeller came together to get a person off the ground and moving through the air! After the world's first flight of a piloted and powered heavier-than-air machine by Wilbur, which lasted no more than 12 seconds, the brothers had three more flights that day. The furthest was 260 metres (284 yards) in 59 seconds.

ONWARDS AND UPWARDS

From these humble beginnings, international air travel was born. Planes quickly became bigger, better, faster and more powerful. Then came the biggest advance in **aviation** since the Wright brothers: the invention of the jet engine by an

Concorde on the runway

Englishman, Sir Frank Whittle, patented in 1930. Instead of air being 'sucked' through a plane's propellers, it could be sucked through fan-like engines, pulling bigger planes at far faster speeds. In 1976, Concorde went into service as the world's first supersonic passenger plane – travelling faster than the speed of sound. The helicopter, meanwhile, had become a reality too. A great many people had a go at building one at the beginning of the twentieth century, but the Americans Emile Berliner and his son Henry built a helicopter which was probably the first aircraft supported by its powered **rotors** to make a genuine, controlled flight. The first truly, 100 per cent successful helicopter was a machine with twin rotors built by the German engineer Heinrich Focke and flown in 1936. Three years later, Russian-born American Igor Sikorsky flew a practical single-rotor helicopter. Helicopters were here to stay.

BY THE SEAT OF THE PANTS

In flight, safety is everything and the ejection seat, invented by Sir James Martin in the 1940s, still saves pilots' lives today. A pull-handle releases the glass canopy above the pilot's head and ejects the seat through the opening. Small parachutes slow the seat down, then a secondary, larger parachute opens, pulling the pilot free from the seat and carrying him to the ground. This is an example of a brilliantly simple idea amazingly executed.

AMAZING ADVANCES

Today, people not only fly through the skies but also in space. Although it takes off by being given a piggyback by a rocket, the space shuttle looks and lands like an ordinary fixed-wing plane. Now, nowhere in the world is more than 24 hours away. Many people also take flying as a passenger in a jumbo jet for granted. The jumbo – real name Boeing 747 – is currently the largest passenger plane in the air. Amazingly, the length of one of its wings is almost the distance of the first flight of the Wright brothers' *Flyer*! In 2007, the A380 will be the largest passenger plane in service with a staggering 50 per cent more floor space than the jumbo!

747

← Wrights' flight! →

THE GUN

26 October 1881, O.K. Corral, Tombstone, Arizona, USA

Doc Holliday, Wyatt Earp and his two brothers face the Clanton gang of suspected cattle rustlers at the start of what is to become one of the most famous gunfights in history: the gunfight at the O.K. Corral. Three of the Clantons won't live to see another day, two of the Earps will be wounded. Doc Holliday and Wyatt Earp will pass into legend . . .

HUNTER GATHERERS

The first weapons used by humans – back in the days of prehistory – were probably rocks and large sticks. You can do a lot of damage with a big rock, but I don't recommend you try it. Later came clubs, spears, axes and bows and arrows. In the early days, most weapons were probably used to hunt animals, not for attacking each other.

TRUE CRAFTSMANSHIP

About 11,000 years ago, people settled down to become the first farmers (rather than being constantly on the move, hunting animals and gathering berries) and had time to concentrate on improving their weapons. The heads of early spears and arrows were made from flint but, later, copper and bronze were used. To begin with, axes and spears were 'tangled' – the pointy heads were bound to the handles or hafts with leather strips or string. By the end of the **Bronze Age**, however, they were fitted in place with proper sockets. By the **Iron Age**, weapons were skilfully made and, often, beautifully decorated. The more important you were, the grander your sword, dagger, helmet and shield.

DIFFERENT TIMESCALES

What type of weapons people used and when depended very much on what part of the world you came from. As long ago as c 1485 BC – that's about 3,485 years ago – Egyptians were riding two-wheeled war chariots, for example. There was nothing similar going on in Europe at the time. In c 500 BC – yup, about 2,500 years ago – the ancient Greeks had triple-decker warships! In 600 – still 1,400 years ago – the Byzantine navy used 'Greek fire', a terrifying flaming liquid fired from tubes!

THE MIGHT OF THE ROMANS

The ancient Romans – whose massive empire was at its height under Emperor Trajan (AD 98–117) – had some very impressive weapons and tactics too. Their soldiers wore uniforms with plenty of flexible body armour and helmets and either a *gladius* short-sword if on horseback or a *pugio* dagger if on foot. They also carried spears. Bigger weapons included siege towers – wooden towers on wheels which, packed with soldiers, could be pushed against the wall of an enemy's defences, allowing the Romans to swarm out and over the top. They had battering rams (to knock down gates) and wooden-framed catapult machines too. These catapults could fire stones a distance of 30 metres (92 feet)!

VIKING ATTACK!

Later came the **Dark Ages**, the time of the Vikings and Saxons in Europe, when, in many ways, things seemed much more primitive than what had gone before. The Vikings were an impressively fierce warrior people (though they rarely, if *ever*, had horns on their helmets, whatever anyone might tell you). They had huge double-edged swords and frightening battleaxes, and must have been a terrifying sight as they approached your shore in a Viking longboat, complete with a figurehead carved like a frightening beast. Only important Saxons had swords. Most foot soldiers had much more basic weapons. King Harold's Saxon army, who faced the invading William the Conqueror's Norman army at the Battle of Hastings in 1066, included many peasants armed with nothing more than rocks and sticks (as in prehistoric times)!

NEW AND IMPROVED

The big advance in weapons came in the Middle Ages in Europe, with the incredible improvement on the age-old idea of the bow and arrow. Now there was the longbow and the crossbow. The longbow remained more like the traditional bow and arrow but was almost as tall as the **archer** who fired it, and it used steel-tipped arrows. It could kill an enemy soldier at 91 metres (100 yards). The crossbow was more of a machine. Imagine a bow on its side, with a wooden shaft running down the middle where the arrow goes. When the bowstring is pulled back, it's held in place on the shaft and an arrow slipped into position. Aim, pull the trigger, and the arrow fires. It was impressive and lethal, and something the Chinese had been using since as long ago as c 400 BC!

PROS AND CONS

A crossbow's arrow could travel far greater distances than a longbow's arrow, and do far more damage . . . but they took much longer to load. To pull the bowstring tight, some crossbows needed special winding machines! The reason why so many castles had cross-shaped slit windows was so that both longbows and crossbows could be used. A longbow could be fired from the vertical slit and a crossbow from the horizontal.

'BOOM!'

The biggest change in European weaponry, though, was undoubtedly the introduction of gunpowder: an explosive mixture of potassium nitrate, charcoal and sulphur. This was the first explosive known to humans. A barrel on its own might blow a hole in a wall . . . in the barrel of a weapon it could fire even more deadly **projectiles**! The original recipe for gunpowder was probably concocted in China, with the earliest-known formula published there in 1045. At that time, the Chinese were more interested in using it to make firecrackers rather than weapons, though they were using 'war rockets' in 1232. The formula for gunpowder can be found in the writings of the thirteenth-century English monk Roger Bacon (the same Roger Bacon who came up with some brilliant thoughts on aeroplanes on page 70),

and it was probably introduced to the West via the Middle East. The Swedish chemist Alfred Nobel, inventor of dynamite in 1867 and founder of the **Nobel Prizes**, went on to invent ballistite, a smokeless gunpowder, in 1889.

A FLASH IN THE PAN

By 1334, gunpowder was being produced on a large scale in England, and in Germany by 1340. The first, most basic cannon was the bombard. It fired very large stone balls and must have seemed the ultimate weapon in fourteenth-century European warfare – like nothing seen before. By c 1400 matchlock weapons were invented, where the pulling of a trigger didn't fire an arrow but struck a match, which then ignited the 'flash' in the pan of the gun, which, in turn, lit the gunpowder in the barrel, which fired the 'shot' (pellets) . . . at least, that was the idea, but matchlocks weren't terribly reliable. So much could go wrong: the match might not strike, or it might just light the flash in the pan. (And yes, that's where the phrase comes from.) Worse than that, the pistols sometimes exploded.

GUNS! GUNS! GUNS!

By 1458, Leonardo da Vinci (yes, him again) was sketching ideas for multibarrelled machine guns! (A man called Maxim didn't invent the first effective machine gun until 1883. It fired 500 bullets per minute.) In 1593 came the first flintlock pistol, though the safest, and most reliable,

Maxim (crouching) with his machine gun, c 1880

version was probably invented by the Frenchman Martin Le Bourgeoys in the 1620s. Flintlocks remained popular right up until the 1830s. Instead of the match, the flash was lit by the spark of striking flints. With such pistols, the gunpowder and shot had to be poured down the barrel and tamped into place with a ramrod. Special flintlocks included grenade launches. Grenades aren't a modern invention. How do you think the grenadiers originally got their name?

THE SOUND OF PERCUSSION

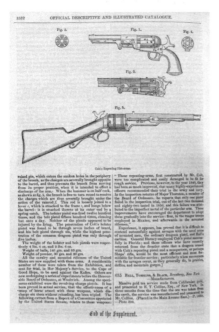

Colt's repeating firearms, 1851

In 1807, percussion lock pistols were invented. They fired more quickly and more safely, and it didn't matter so much if they were wet. In early percussion weapons, a small cap of detonator exploded when hit by the gun's hammer, sending a jet of flame to the powder, which fired the ball. Later, the cap, powder and ball were combined to create a single cartridge. Then, in 1836, Samuel Colt patented his revolver: percussion-fired, with a five-chamber cylinder that revolved automatically to line up the next bullet with the barrel. (The first revolver had been invented in 1818, but it was a flintlock with a chamber that had to be turned by hand.) By 1847, the Colt was in general use – this was the same year that the deadly explosive nitroglycerine was discovered.

BOMBS!

The first real air raid – bombing from the air – was in 1915 when Zeppelin airships dropped bombs on London. The first tanks were in action in 1916, with the British Mark 1 on the battlefield of the Somme in France. A year later, the world's first guided missile was launched. Unlike today's hi-tech devices, it was a biplane on autopilot, packed with 136 kg (300 lb) of explosives!

MORE AND MORE FIREPOWER

Since then, everything has snowballed. After the revolver came the semi-automatic – a self-loading handgun firing a shot at the pull of the trigger, and the automatic – a self-loader which fires repeatedly once the trigger is pulled. Both rely on a magazine full of cartridges clipped into the handle of the weapon. Today, military personnel, with their armoured cars, tanks, ships and planes, are armed to the teeth! With the discovery of the power of the atom   which you can read all about in *WOW: Discoveries that changed the world* – came atomic weapons. There was the A-Bomb, the H-bomb and then intercontinental ballistic missiles: weapons powerful enough to destroy Earth and everyone on it. Whether you see that as an advance on using big rocks and sticks is, of course, a matter of opinion, but guns and the weapons that followed have undeniably changed our lives. For those of us living in a world of guns, it's

virtually impossible to imagine what it would be like without them. There would probably have been far fewer wars, and what wars there still would have been would certainly have resulted in far fewer deaths.

PRINTING

1455, MAINZ, GERMANY

Johann Gutenberg carefully lifts out the piece of paper from his printing press, the ink still wet. His hands shake slightly. He is holding the final page of his 1,282-page book. He has used over 400,000 separate letters to create the very first printed Bible in the world.

Gutenberg's press, c 1430

THE BIRTH OF HISTORY

The birth of writing was the birth of history, literally. Anything that happened before writing is known as prehistory, which is where we get the word 'prehistoric' from. The earliest form of record-keeping was probably nicks out of a stick or bone, one nick representing one animal owned. True writing developed in a place called Sumer (which is in what is now Iraq) about 5,500 years ago, and a little later in ancient Egypt. Very few people in these societies could read or write. In Egypt, this was the special job of people called scribes. It took them about twelve years to learn all they needed to know.

IMPRESSIVE BEGINNINGS

Early forms of writing weren't written on paper but carved into wax tablets or on to stone monuments or buildings. An ancient library of wax tablets was found in Elba, Iraq. (Yup, they even had libraries back then . . . but not with any of my books in them.) The earliest forms of printing are ancient too. Stamps – not the things you lick 'n' stick but the things you stamp with – are probably the earliest examples, and were used in Babylonia. A design or symbol would be cut into stone and then used as a **signet** to leave an impression in clay as a seal, or rubbed with an early form of ink (made from mud or natural pigment) and stamped to leave a mark. Some stamp or signet stones were set in rings, worn by important people who used them as their signatures.

HANDMADE

For a long, long time books throughout the world were, however, written by hand. If you wanted more than one copy of a book, it had to be copied out, letter for letter.

This didn't stop the ancient Romans publishing over 5,000 copies of the same book – each one having been copied out by one of a group of unpaid, but **literate**, slaves! Some of the most famous handwritten books that survive today, however, were written in medieval monasteries. These are called illuminated manuscripts.

EAST IS EAST

Printing in the East and printing in the West developed in different ways and at different speeds. This was at a time when East and West were cut off from one another, so it wasn't so easy to pinch ideas and inventions off each other! The first form of printing to develop in China was for printing pictures and designs on to clothing in the 1st century AD. By the second century AD, these skills had been used to print text – words – too.

ON THE BLOCK

The method the Chinese used was block printing, where whole pages or words were carved into a piece of wood, back to front, so, when pressed on to paper, they would come out the right way around. In AD 972, the sacred

Buddhist scriptures, called the *Tipitaka*, were printed using wooden blocks. They were more than a staggering 130,000 pages long!

MOVABLE TYPE

The printing process that was to revolutionize the West in the fifteenth century – some 1,300 years later – was actually invented by a Chinaman in the second century. Rather than carving out a whole page of type on a single block, why not use movable type, where you could rearrange the characters to make up different words and sentences and use them again and again? he argued. The problem was that, unlike English – where you'd only need an alphabet of 26 letters, the numerals 0 to 9 and a handful of punctuation marks to make up all the words, numbers and sentences you'd ever need – the Chinese language uses up to 40,000 separate characters! It's not surprising that the invention proved unpopular in China and was soon dropped.

PAPER! PAPER!

An important part of the printing process was what you printed *on*. In the West, people wrote on papyrus (made of woven reeds) and vellum (a tissue from the hides of skinned animals). Papyrus was too fragile to print on and vellum too expensive. When the Chinese invented paper, in about AD 105, they'd come up with a tough, cheap alternative to both. Paper could be made from bark, straw, leaves and even rags!

LATER, IN THE WEST

The invention of paper didn't reach the West until the twelfth century, and didn't really spread throughout Europe until two hundred years later. By the middle of the fifteenth, though, there was paper, paper everywhere – and along came Johann Gutenberg of Mainz, in Germany.

Johann Gutenberg

Gutenberg is said to have invented his printing press in 1450 and to have started work on the Gutenberg Bible in 1455. (Other Western countries have since laid claim to *their* inventing movable type before Gutenberg but, even if that's true, they hadn't made such a good job of it as Gutenberg. His Bible – copies of which still survive today – are so beautiful that they look very like genuine, hand-written and hand-drawn illuminated manuscripts.) In next to no time, printing presses were springing up everywhere. William Caxton set up his printing press in England in 1476 and many Britons imagine that it was Caxton who invented this method of printing. How wrong they are – and you know better.

93

William Caxton in his workshop

THE EARLY PRESSES

The Chinese had simply hand-pressed their wooden blocks of type, covered with water-based paint, on to paper. Western printers always used more permanent, oil-based paint, and built presses that could screw down the type hard and flat on to the paper. (The paper was placed on a 'bed' and the type was pressed down on to it with the 'platen'.) This was a slow business. Only one side of a page could be printed at a time, and the platen had to be screwed up and down between each printing. In the seventeenth century, someone had the bright idea of adding springs so that the platen could be raised and lowered much faster. Iron presses were introduced in about 1800. Up until then, all presses had been wooden. Now levers replaced the huge screws that pressed the platen against the bed. These presses were much bigger, so many pages could be printed on to one huge sheet of paper, which was then folded and cut into the pages of a book.

LEAPS AND BOUNDS

Early Western printing presses were mostly used for religious or worthy works. As printing got cheaper, thousands of pamphlets were printed, putting forward every political point of view under the sun. More and more newspapers cropped up, requiring bigger and bigger machines. In the nineteenth century, steam-powered presses appeared, along with presses that could print *both* sides of the paper at once. In 1863, the American inventor William A. Bullock patented the first newspaper press to print from enormous rolls of paper rather than flat sheets. By 1871, another American, Richard March Hoe, had invented the continuous roll press, which could print a staggering 18,000 newspapers an hour!

HOT METAL

The invention of the Linotype typesetting machine in 1886 and the commercial use of Monotype typesetting machines in the 1890s really speeded up the setting of the metal type – putting the correct letters in place ready for the printing presses. The Linotype could cast whole lines of type at once; the Monotype produced single letters. The advantage of this second method was that the letters could be used again and again, and at very high speed. Then, in

Lithographic printing press, c.1860

the 1950s, along came the first phototypesetting machines. Instead of setting actual type in metal, they produced photographic negatives of the type which could then, like ordinary photography, be used to make plates but, in this case, **lithographic plates**. By the 1960s, phototypesetting pretty much had done away with a printing process that had been perfectly good for about 500 years.

COMPUTER MAGIC

Then, suddenly, the whole printing world was turned upside down *again*. This time by the invention of computers. Computers can do everything from setting type to scanning and retouching photographs, putting everything together on a single piece of film or even straight on to a printing plate. Late twentieth-century advances in desktop publishing meant that it was even possible for people to print out high-quality documents from their own personal PCs at home. With the introduction of the Internet and email, the need to print out so much information on to paper has been greatly reduced. Nowadays there are many newspapers and magazines that don't actually exist on paper but simply online, on screen. We've come a long, long way since Gutenberg and the Chinese. Today, a single copy of a Sunday newspaper contains more words and information than the average fourteenth-, fifteenth-, sixteenth-, or even seventeenth-century person had access to in their lives.

THE COMPUTER

World War II is over and the work at Bletchley Park, home to Project X, is at an end too. On the orders of the prime minister, Winston Churchill, all evidence of the **classified** operations carried out here are being destroyed. And that includes the world's first programmable computer – a computer so top secret that the rest of the world won't hear about it until 1974, almost thirty years later!

The 'Colossus' Computer, Bletchley Park

CALCULATING MACHINES

In the days before PCs, email and the Internet, a computer's main function was to compute (work out) numbers and data – hence the name. For that reason, you could argue that the abacus (where different beads on a frame represent tens, units, hundreds and so on) is an early computer; *very* early, in fact. It's been around for 5,000 years (since 3000 BC). But that's not a proper computer though, is it? Is it? Then what about the German William Schickard's 'calculator clock' of 1623? He claimed it could multiply any two six-digit numbers together, which is more than my calculator can do – there's no room in the display window for the answer. Schickard's calculator clock was reconstructed in 1960, and it worked. Then, in 1642, there was Frenchman Blaise Pascal's 'Pascaline' machine – which wasn't such a success because it kept on jamming. (This probably pleased a lot of locals, by the way. Pascal had built it to help his dad work out how much money he needed to take off people, in his job as a tax collector!) In

1673, another German, this time one Gottfried Leibniz, built a highly successful calculating machine that not only multiplied, added and subtracted but divided too – could that be seen as an early computer?

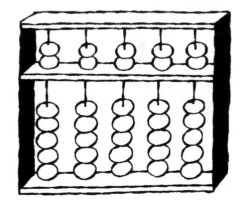

BABBAGE, THE MAIN MAN

Charles Babbage, 1843

Whatever the answer, most experts agree – yes, *agree* – that one person is the 'father of the computer' and that person was Englishman Charles Babbage (1792–1871). Babbage had a brilliant mind. The British government actually gave him £17,000 to build a very complicated mechanical calculator which he called a 'difference engine'. That was a *very* big sum of money back then. But, after ten years, the money ran out and they wouldn't give him any more. Although all of Babbage's calculations had been right, his mechanical calculator kept on coming up with the wrong answers. The reason for this was simple: ninteenth-century technology wasn't advanced enough to build the kinds of machine he wanted to build. He was even having to invent the tools that he needed to use to make certain parts of the 'engine'!

ANOTHER BRILLIANT FAILURE

Abandoning his 'difference engine', Babbage invented his 'analytical engine' in 1833. This was an even more brilliant invention, but one he couldn't even start to build, let alone finish! It was a machine that could be programmed to do lots of different functions, that could store the results ('remember' them) and then print them out on paper – if only he could actually build one! What Babbage was trying to create was a machine that does exactly what electronic computers do today. He was, sadly, a genius who got nowhere.

ANOTHER WORLD FIRST

Lady Ada Lovelace, 1840

Babbage was ably assisted by Ada Byron, Countess of Lovelace (**aka** Lady Ada Lovelace), another person with an amazing mind. Lady Ada was the world's first true computer programmer! Methods she worked out for programming Babbage's 'analytical engine' were early versions of the language actually used in modern computers, and involved cards punched with a series of holes. Hole-punch cards and, later, strips were to become a vital part in computers (but were originally used to programme looms to weave certain patterns). And don't forget the secret of how the pianola played its tunes on page 18. Sadly, Babbage spent 37 years working on the

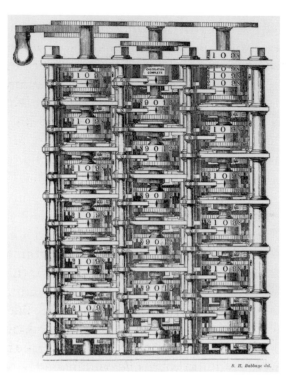

Charles Babbage's Difference Engine No.1

'analytical engine' with no end result, and Lady Ada – a gambler – died penniless. In 1991 the Science Museum in London built a copy of the difference engine using modern, machine-tooled components, in time for the 200th anniversary of Babbage's birth in 1792. It contained over 4,000 parts, weighed over 3 tonnes and worked *perfectly*.

ON THE HOLE

In 1886, American inventor Herman Hollerith devised a successful method of recording information using the hole-punch card method, and built a machine to 'read' them. Information from the 1890 US **census** was recorded on to hole-punch cards, and his tabulating machines could then analyse the statistics. Hollerith formed a company in 1896 with the snappy title of the Computing-Tabulating-Recording Company. It grew and grew and grew and, in 1924, changed its name to the International Business Machines Corporation – or IBM, for short.

COMPUTER GIANTS

Throughout most of its existence, IBM has been the biggest computer corporation in the world. Its first chairperson was a man called Thomas Watson (though not, as far as I'm aware, the same Thomas Watson who was shouted at by Alexander Graham Bell back on page 3). As far as Watson was concerned, the most important thing his employees could do was to *think*.

THE BREAKTHROUGH

1941 saw the construction of the world's first all-electric program-mable computer: Colossus. Well, in fact, only very few people actually *saw* the construction of the machine, let alone the finished result. Designed and built by Englishman Tommy Flowers, one of a team at Bletchley Park, Woking, under Alan Turing – brilliant

Enigma cypher machine, c 1930s

103

mathematician, codebreaker and pioneer of computer theory – Colossus was top, top, *top* secret and built to crack the Nazi's codes in World War II. In early tests, it could read information off paper tape optically at speeds of up to 60 miles of tape an hour! Colossus was very large, and it relied on electrical **valves**, so got very hot. The computer room was a popular place to work in during the cold winters, but not in hot summers. It was also an excellent place for drying clothes!

SAYING NOTHING

Even after the war, Colossus remained a secret under Britain's **Official Secrets Act**. As late as 1973, a US judge declared – as part of a legal case over a patent – that a computer, completed in 1942 by an American named Atanasoff, was the first – unaware of Tommy Flowers's remarkable achievement. Yet no one could tell the judge that he was wrong! Flowers was a telephone engineer by trade and, after the war, he was unable to tell anyone about his amazing invention and went back to his old job! The secret only came to light in a book published in 1974, which broke the Official Secrets Act.

INCREDIBLE SHRINKING MACHINES

The first all-purpose computer was built from 1943 to 1945 at the University of Pennsylvania in the US and is called ENIAC (short for Electronic Numerical Integrator And Computer). Unlike Colossus, it was designed to do lots of different tasks. Soon, other people were building computers and, because they also relied on valves, these had to be huge too. Then, in 1947, the transistor was invented. It was developed by three Americans – Brattain, Bardeen and Schockley – and had such a big impact on everything from radios to computers that it won them the Nobel Prize for Physics in 1956. Why? Because a tiny transistor did the work of large, easily breakable and heat-creating valves.

CHIPS WITH EVERYTHING

The next big leap came when transistors were, in turn, replaced by **silicon chips** – sometimes called microchips because they're so small – in 1969. This was really the beginning of what we think of as computers today. By 1975, the Altair, the first personal computer, went on sale – not that you'd recognize it as one. Firstly, you had to build it yourself, as it came as a kit! Secondly, it didn't have a screen! Thirdly, there was no '**qwerty**' keyboard! It was all about flicking switches and flashing lights. A version of the BASIC computer-programming language was developed for the Altair by two Harvard University students: Paul Allen and Bill Gates.

A FLOOD OF CHANGES

In 1980, a company called Acorn manufactured BBC computers for the BBC (British Broadcasting Corporation) to go with a programme about computers. The BBC thought they might manage to sell as many as 10,000 computers. In fact, they sold over a million. Next came Sir Clive Sinclair's Sinclair Spectrum computer, another big hit, especially because

A Sinclair ZX Spectrum microcomputer, 1982

it could generate colour graphics on screen. Then, in 1981, came IBM's PC which had the basic look that modern computer **hardware** has today. 1984 saw the Apple company build their Macintosh computer. Apple Macs were easier to use than IBM's PC. They had easy-to-follow icons on screen, and the user could do much less typing-in of commands. In 1985, IBM brought in a similar look, using Windows software designed by Microsoft. This was a company set up by Bill Gates and Paul Allen, who'd dropped out of Harvard by now, with the idea of working towards 'a computer on every desk and in every home'. Today, most computers in the world use Windows and Bill Gates is one of the richest men in the world.

AND NOW?

Computers have changed beyond recognition. A laptop computer, smaller than a briefcase, can perform operations in minutes that an old-fashioned computer, the size of a room, took days to do! Back in 1943, Thomas Watson of IBM didn't think there'd be a need for more than five computers in the whole world. Today, they're in millions of people's homes and some people are even doing their weekly shopping on them! There are computers that can talk, using speech synthesis. There are computers that can listen, using voice recognition.

THE WORLD WIDE WEB

We can't discuss the invention of computers without mentioning the invention of the Internet. As early as the 1960s, computers at military bases across the US were linked to each other in a network. In the 1970s, universities across the US networked their computers and soon universities in other countries were doing it too. By the 1980s, computers from different countries were networked to each other and the Internet was born, but computer users needed to have a specific computer's address before being able to communicate with it. Then, in the 1990s, Tim Berners-Lee, an employee of the Swiss-based physics institute called CERN, invented the world's first browser – a programme which, once given a name or topic to look for, searched the network for it. Now anyone could surf the World Wide Web! Today, there are over 970 million users.

THEY'RE EVERYWHERE!

Computers are remarkable in just how quickly they've changed the way we can do just about everything. Want to get out some money? Use a cashpoint machine. Want to find a book in the library? Use the on-screen catalogue. Want to know the speed a race was run? Check the electronic timekeeper. Want to guide a missile? Pilot a plane? Set the central-heating controls? Book a holiday? Monitor a patient's blood flow and heartbeat? Regulate medication? Record a song? Store a photo? There are computers to do all of these things and more. And will there really soon be a new breed of computers that can think for themselves, like we do? Perhaps you should ask one. Nicely.

GLOSSARY

aka – short for 'also known as'

archer – a soldier using a bow and arrow, longbow or crossbow

aviation – the science of building and flying aircraft

beasts of burden – animals used to work (carry, plough, turn mill wheels, etc.), often donkeys, asses, horses and oxen

Bronze Age – The first prehistoric humans used wood, bone and stone tools and this period was called the Stone Age. Later, they used bronze – a compound of copper and tin. This was the Bronze Age. It began in the Middle East in c 4500 BC, but lasted in Britain from about 2000 BC to 500 BC. It was followed by the Iron Age

c – short for the Latin word 'circa', meaning 'about'. A date marked c means an approximate date; the event occurred around about then

census – an official account of all the people living in a country, made up from answers filled in on questionnaires

classified – to say that a project is classified is shorthand for saying that it has been made a secret by the government, probably for reasons of national security

colliery – a coal mine

compounds – a substance made up of two or more chemical elements that can only be separated with a chemical reaction

convex – bowing outwards

Dark Ages – a period in European history from the late fifth century AD to about 1000 (a thousand years ago)

diaphragm – a thin disc that vibrates when receiving sound-waves, converting them into electrical signals, or which vibrates and produces sound-waves when turning electrical signals into sound

employees – people working for someone. Edison's employees were employed by him. He paid their wages

facsimile – a very accurate copy

hardware – the computer equipment itself, including the monitor, keyboard and hard disc, rather than the software

independently – on your own, without help from others

Iron Age – the period after the Bronze Age, involving the spread of iron weapons and tools, occurring at different times in different parts of the world

lift – gravity is the force that tries to keep everything (including aeroplanes) firmly on the ground. Lift is the upward force that overcomes gravity, keeping planes in the sky. Lift is produced by wings and propeller blades with a special aerofoil shape moving through the air. (Looking at it from the side, an aerofoil wing or propeller blade has a larger curve on its upper surface than its lower surface)

literate – able to read and write

lithographic plates – printing plates where certain areas (in the shapes of the letters) are made ink-receptive, whilst the surrounding areas remain ink-repellent

masses – the mass population. Lots of us lot!

mercury – sometimes called quicksilver, a liquid metal often found in thermometers

misconception – a strongly held belief that isn't, in fact, true

newsreel – news captured on film and shown in a weekly news round-up at the cinema, in the days before television was so popular

Nobel Prize – an annual prize given for outstanding contributions to physics, chemistry, physiology, medicine, literature, peace and now economics too. Awarded by an international committee in Sweden (except for the peace prize, awarded in Norway)

obsolete – outdated, outmoded, yesterday's model

Official Secrets Act – a British law designed to prevent people from giving away important government secrets

optical – using light

parachute – a large piece of cloth, attached to a person by thin ropes, designed to open out in a canopy, slow down the person – who has jumped or been ejected from a plane – and bring him or her safely to the ground

patent – a legal permit designed to stop others stealing your invention. A patent prevents everyone else from making or selling the invention you have patented

pedestrians – people going around on foot

Pony Express – a mail delivery service in the American West, using relays of horse and riders. It was at its height from Missouri to California in 1860–1861, and surprisingly fast

persevere – to stick at doing something

projectiles – any objects fired from a gun. These could be large iron balls, tiny lead pellets and, later, bullets and shells

propeller – a series of blades, shaped like small aerofoil wings on their sides. A propeller creates lift, sucking itself (and the aeroplane) along – propelling the plane forwards – pushing out air behind it

qwerty – a 'qwerty' keyboard is a standard English keyboard with the top line of letters beginning with the letters 'q', 'w', 'e', 'r', 't' and 'y'

revolution – one complete turn of a circle. 'Revolutions per minute' are the number of times an object completes a revolution in a minute

rotors – the rotating blades of a helicopter, fixed to a central stem. The rotors produce thrust and lift to make the machine fly

satellites – human-made devices,

orbiting the Earth, sending and receiving communications

signet – a seal used to stamp documents, often set in a (signet) ring

silicon chips – sometimes called microchips; tiny pieces of silicon with electronic circuits printed on them

software – computer programmes and operating systems, rather than the actual hardware

sprocket – a wheel with 'teeth' on either rim, designed to catch in holes down the side of a strip of film to pull it through the camera or projector

stylus – a pointed instrument. Later, a stylus came to mean the needle of a record player, often tipped with a diamond

valves – vacuum devices used to control a flow of electrons in electric circuits

vapour – a gas, usually one that's been changed from a liquid or a solid

vibration – the act of something vibrating (rapidly moving back and forth, quivering)

Index

PHILIP ARDAGH

Imagine the unimaginable: a world without electricity, genetics, penicillin, nuclear weapons or even plastic. Have you ever wondered how such things were discovered?

From theories of gravity and relativity to X-rays and DNA, this book is packed with facts and photographs that look at discoveries that – for good or for bad – have made the world what it is today.

Eureka!

PHiLiP ArdagH'S book OF
ABSOLUTELY
USELESS
LISTS
fOR aBSOLUTELY EVERY DaY Of THE YEaR

After years of obsessive fact-hoarding, Philip Ardagh has plundered the deepest corners of his brain to bring you this ridiculously named, reassuringly chunky book, jam-packed full of eye-openingly absurd facts, lies, half-truths, thoughts, suggestions and musings, with more footnotes than an orchestra of millipedes.

The lists include:
- Possessors of Notable Moustaches (Real or Otherwise)
- What MI5 Looks for When Recruiting
- Basic Requirements for Being a Pirate Captain
- Animal Breakouts

A selected list of titles available from Macmillan Children's Books

The prices shown below are correct at the time of going to press.
However, Macmillan Publishers reserves the right to show new retail prices
on covers, which may differ from those previously advertised.

Philip Ardagh

Philip Ardagh's Book of Absolutely Useless Lists	978-0-330-43417-1	£6.99
WOW: discoveries that changed the world	978-0-330-44453-8	£3.99
WOW: events that changed the world	978-0-330-44874-1	£3.99
WOW: ideas that changed the world	978-0-330-44875-8	£3.99
The Truth About Love	978-0-330-41009-0	£3.99
The Truth About Fairies	978-0-330-44285-5	£3.99
The Truth About Cats	978-1-405-06710-2	£5.99

All Pan Macmillan titles can be ordered from our website,
www.panmacmillan.com, or from your local bookshop
and are also available by post from:

Bookpost, PO Box 29, Douglas, Isle of Man IM99 1BQ
Credit cards accepted. For details:
Telephone: 01624 677237
Fax: 01624 670923
Email: bookshop@enterprise.net
www.bookpost.co.uk

Free postage and packing in the United Kingdom